Les Chutes de Grand-Sault
The Grand Falls

Wendy Koenig

Copyright © 2010 Wendy Koenig
All rights reserved

Published by Cadillac Press
185 Drummond St. Rd.
Drummond, NB E3Y 1V9
Canada

Printed by Lulu.com

This book, photos, or any other parts thereof, may not be reproduced in any form without permission of the author. The scanning, uploading and distribution of this book via the Internet or via any other means without the permission of the publisher is illegal and punishable by law.

2 4 6 8 10 9 7 5 3 1
FIRST EDITION

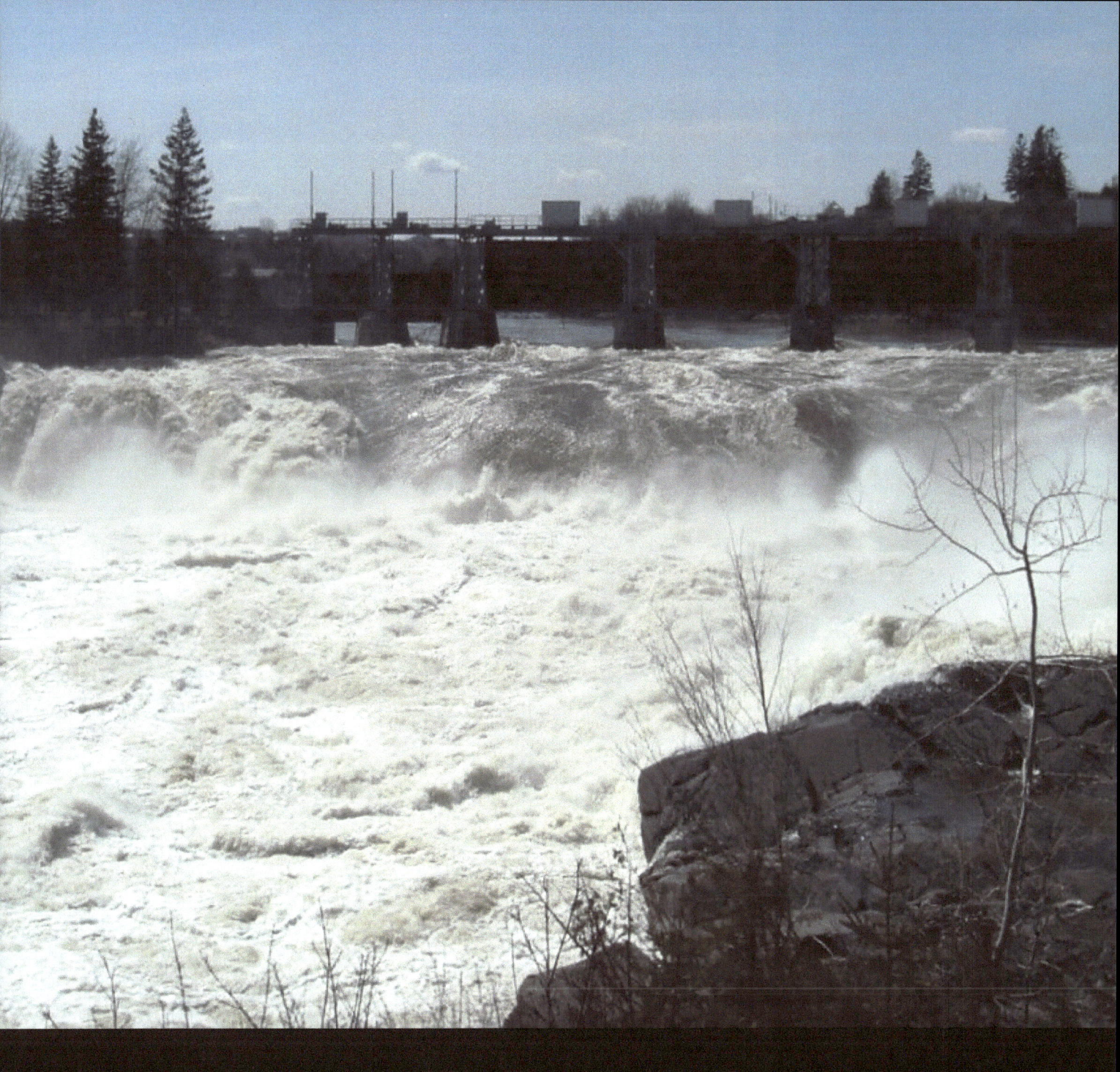

En Printemps
Early Spring

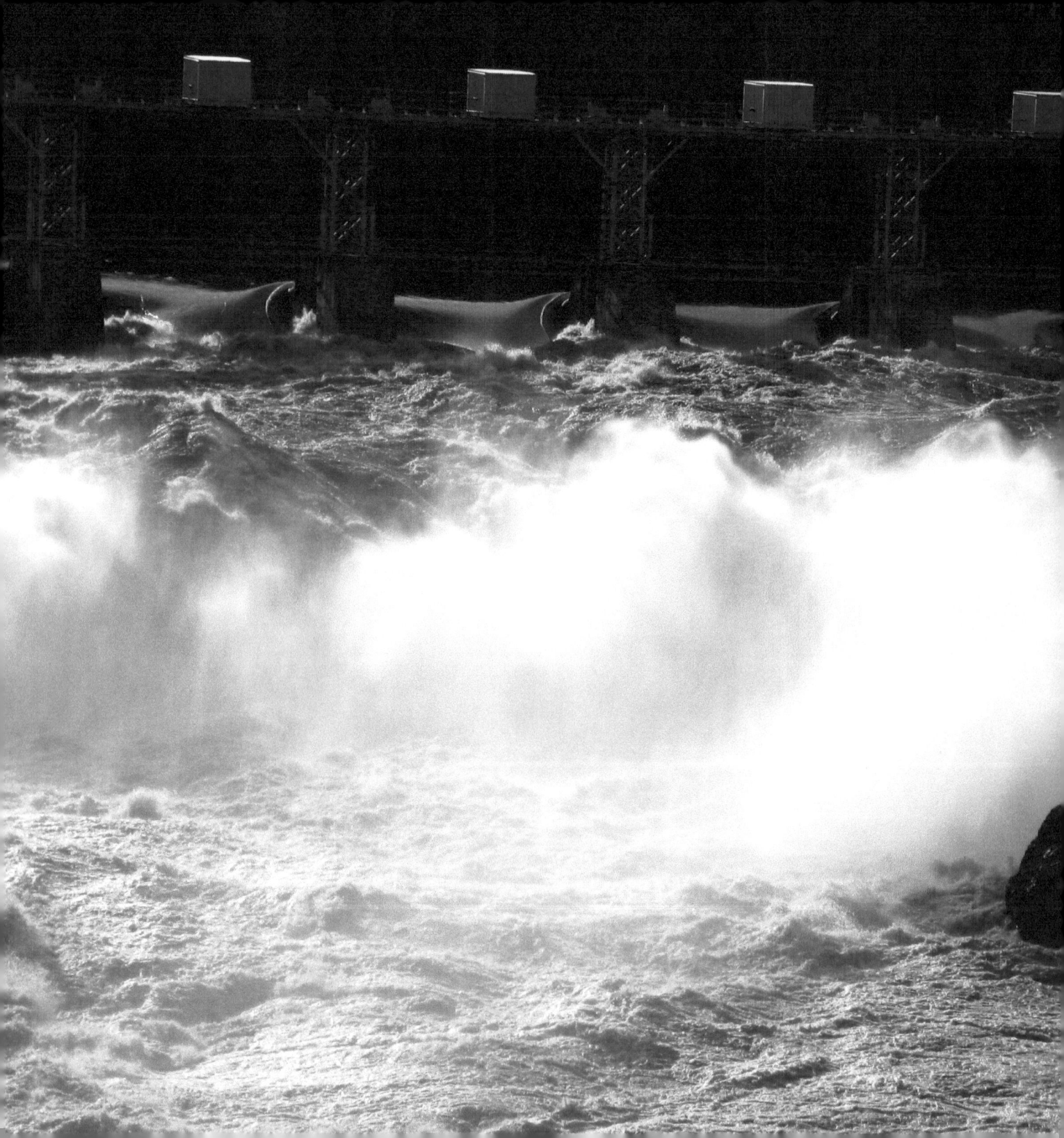

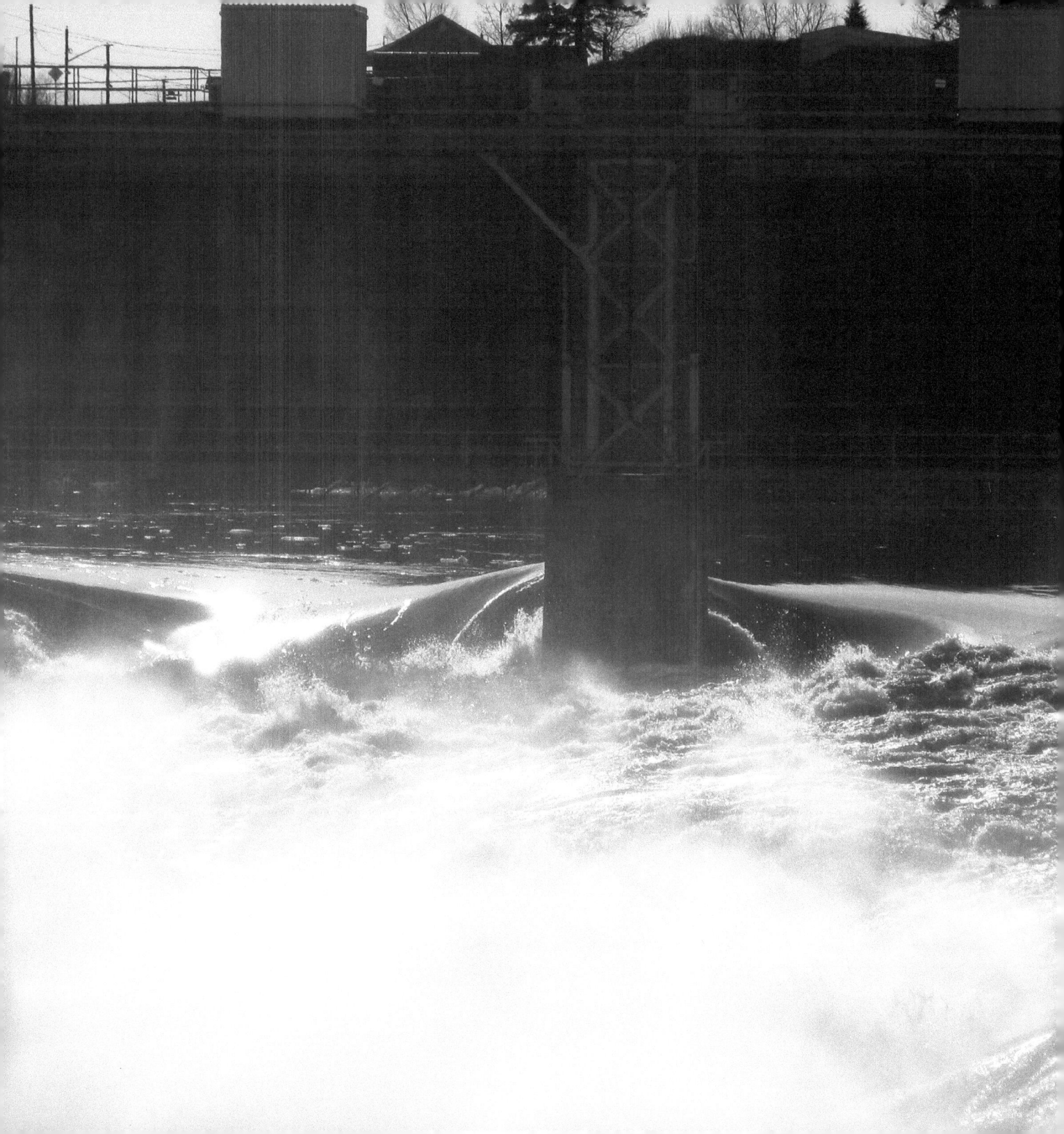

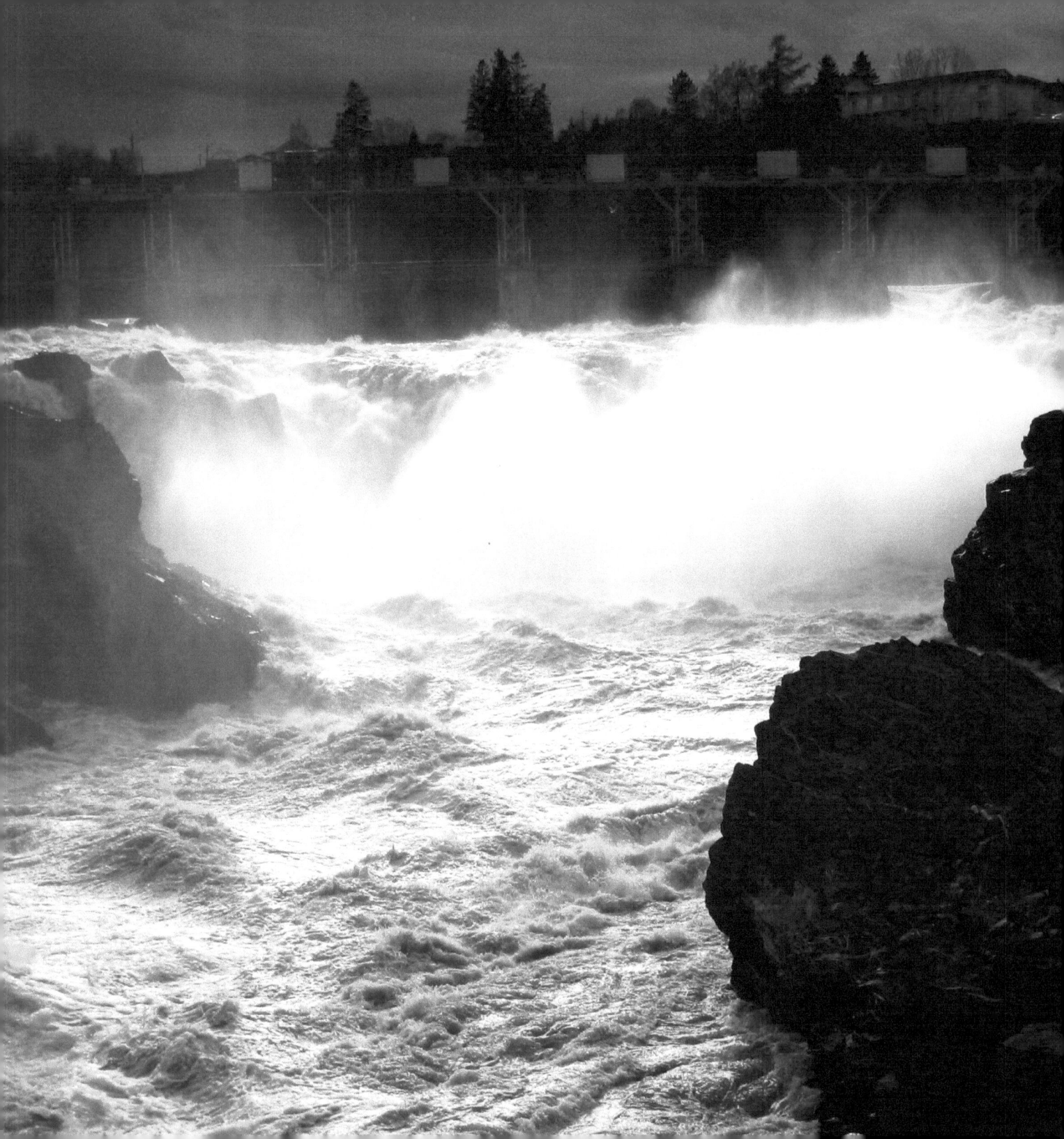

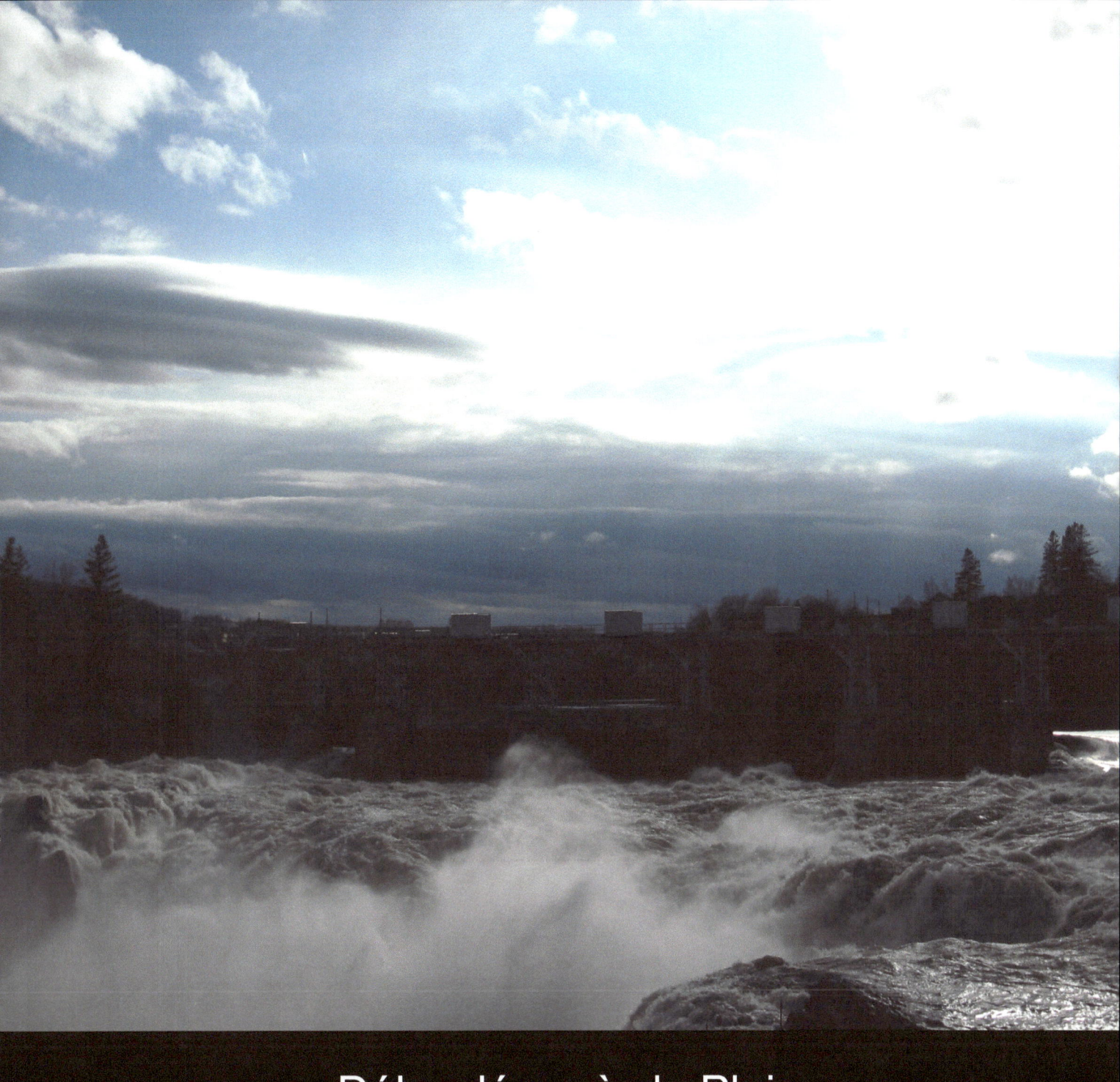

Débordé après la Pluie
Swollen after a Rain

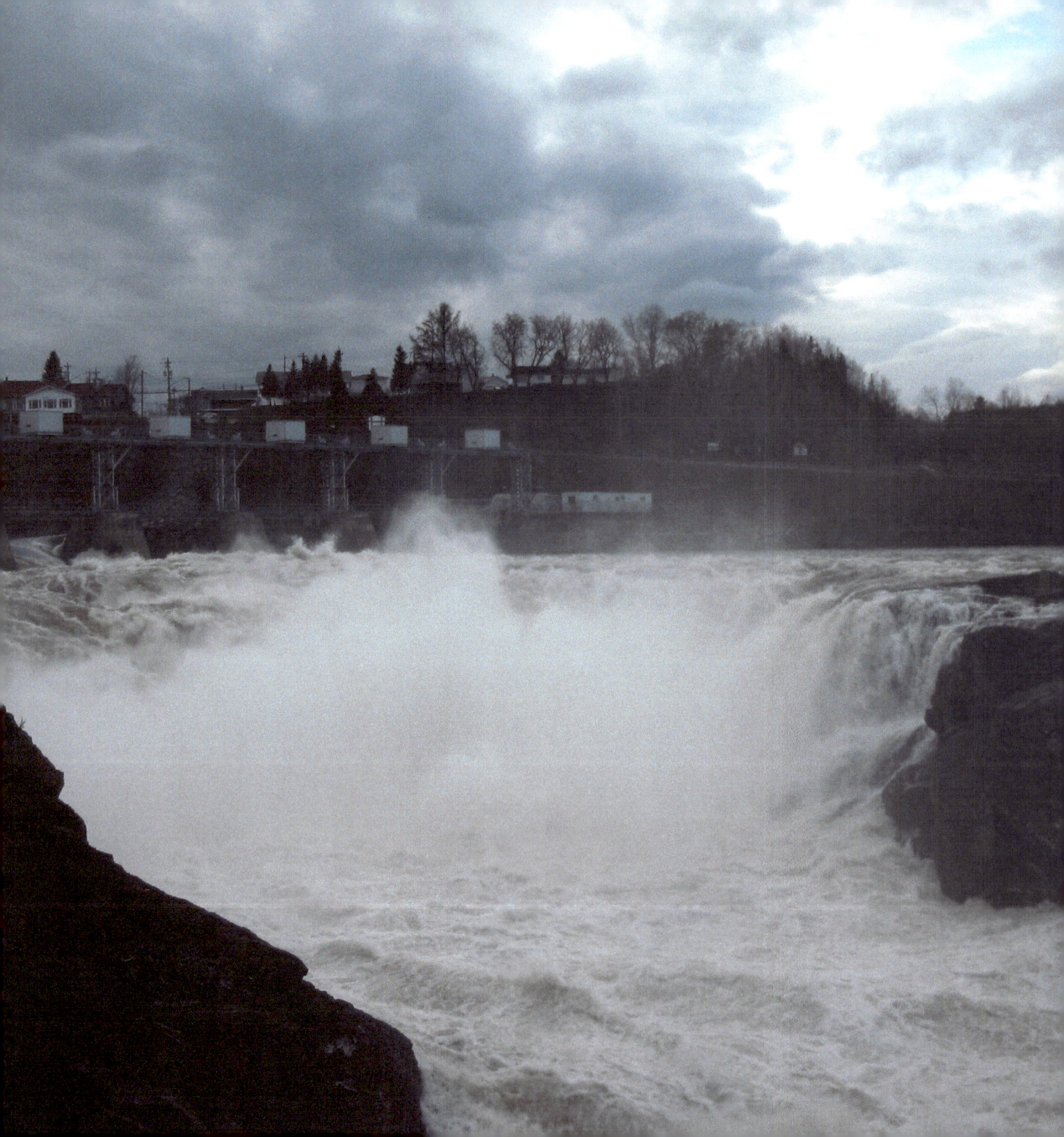

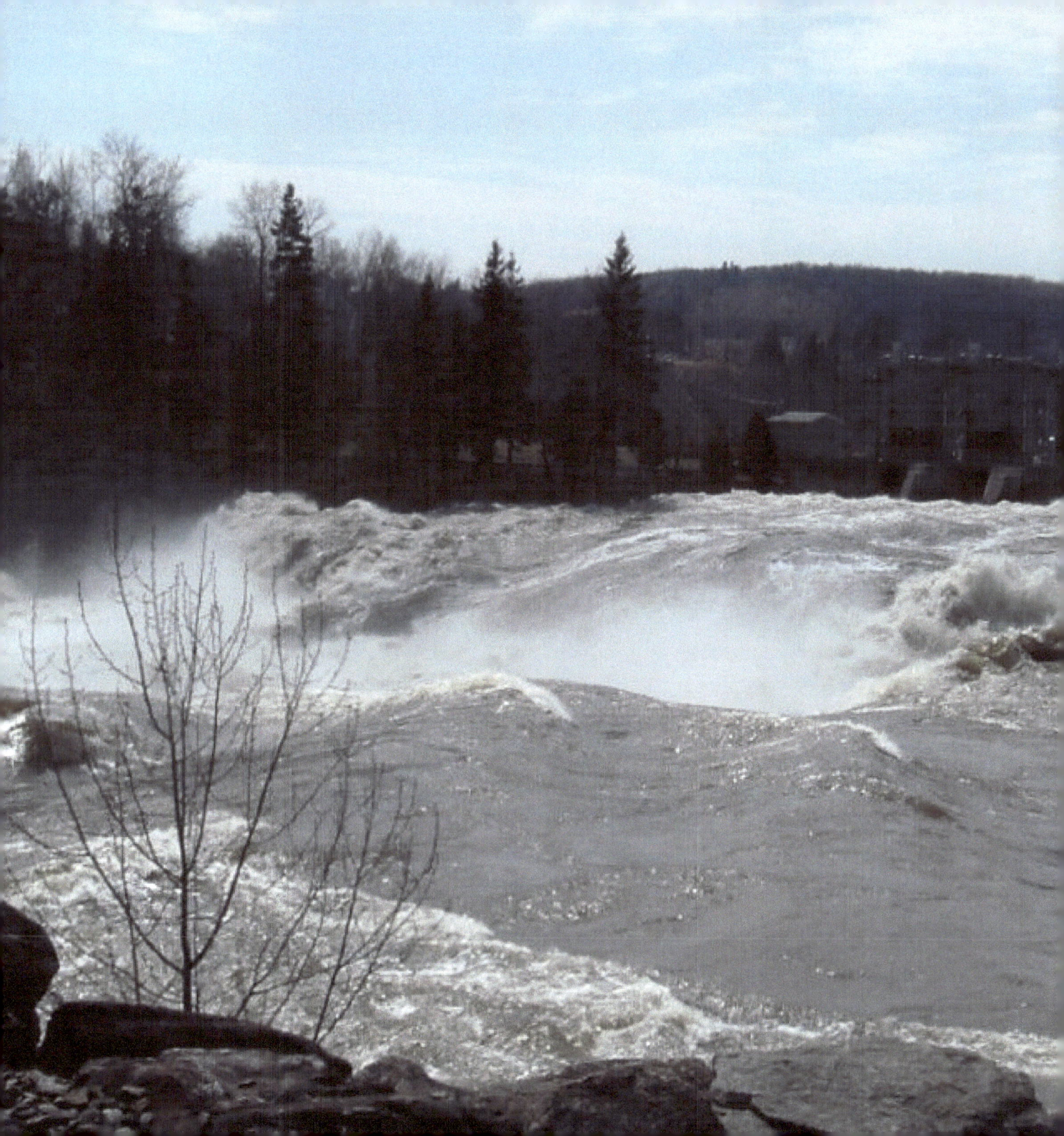

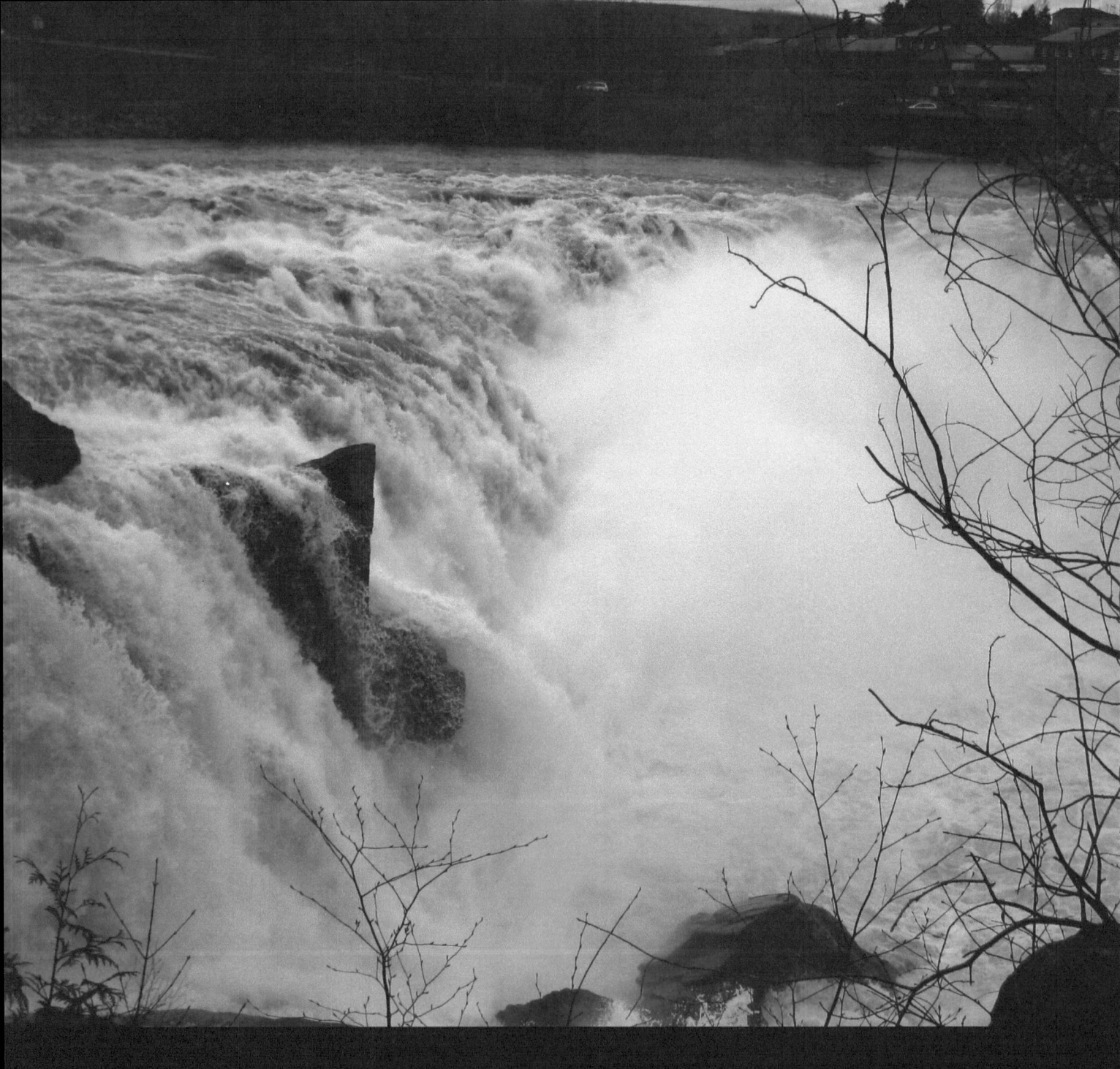

Les Chutes à Travers
Across the Falls

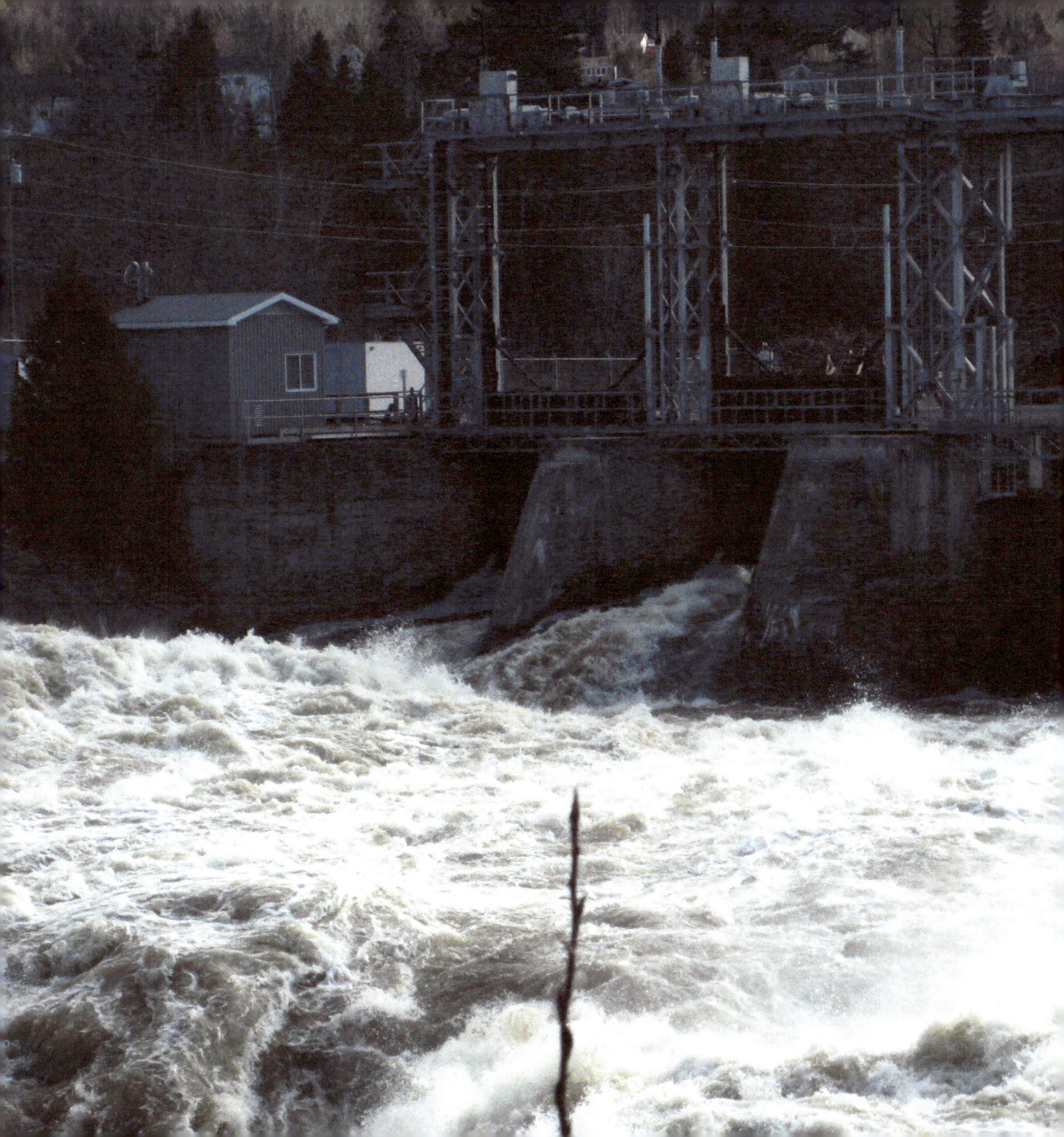

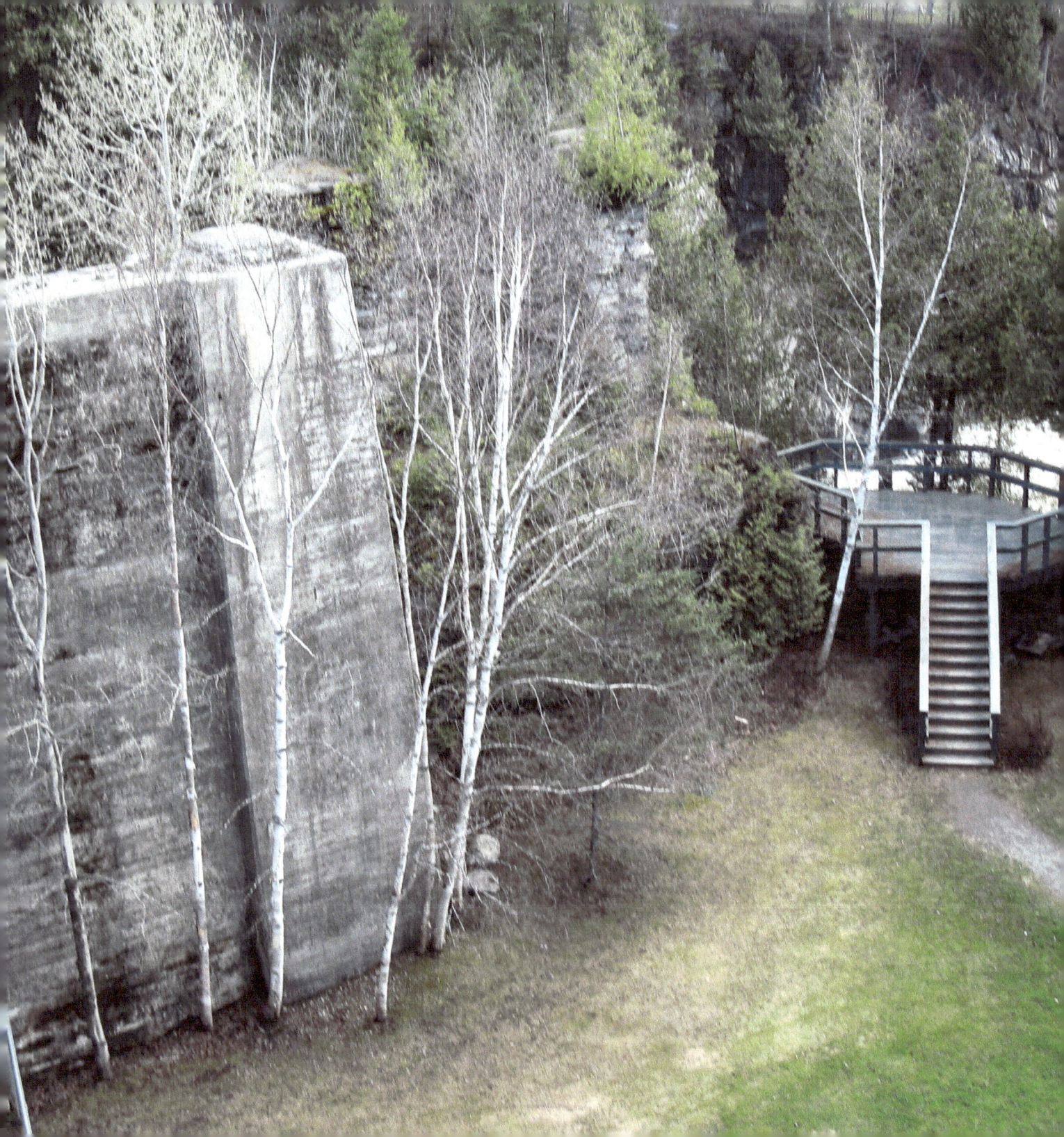

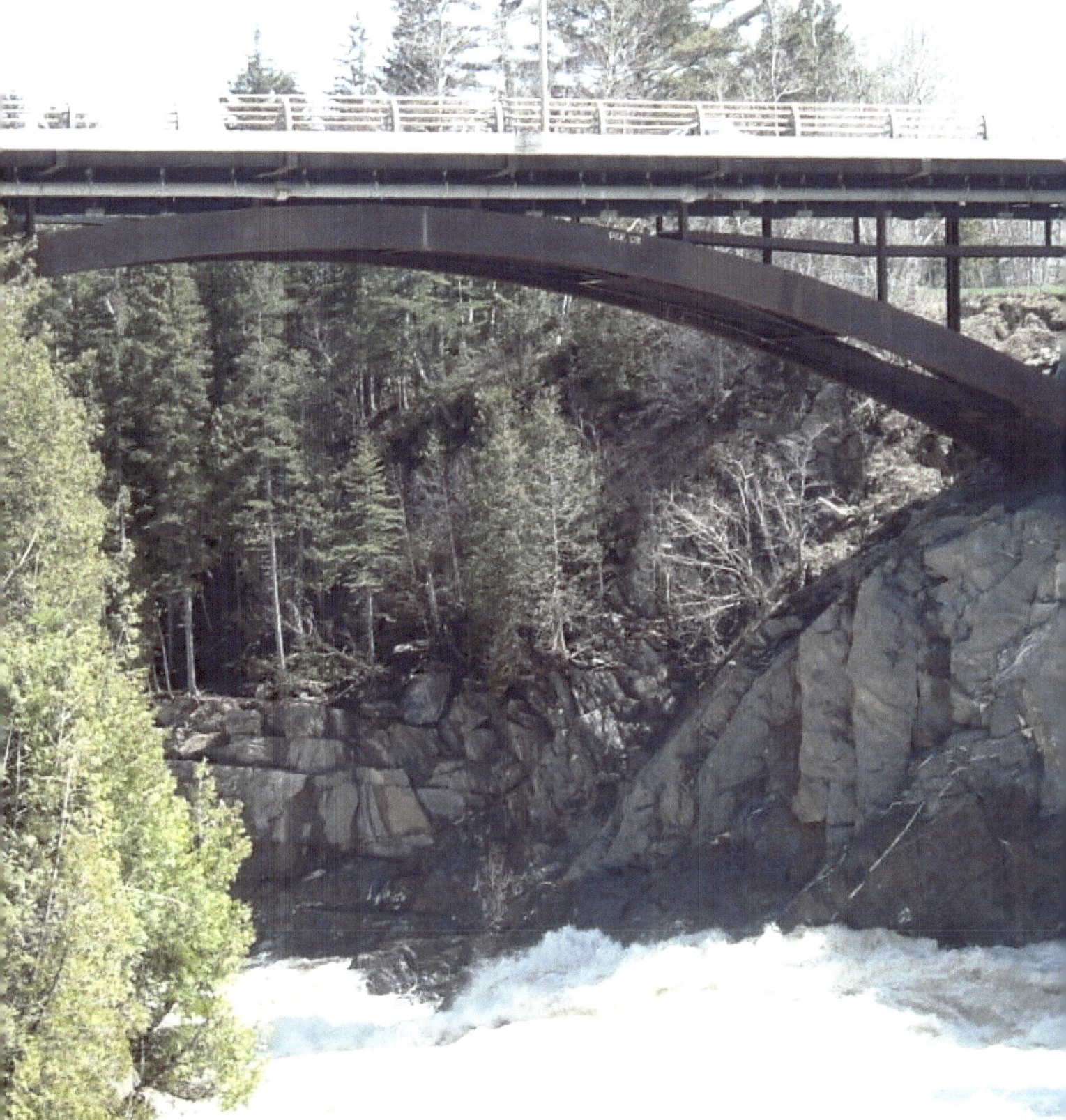

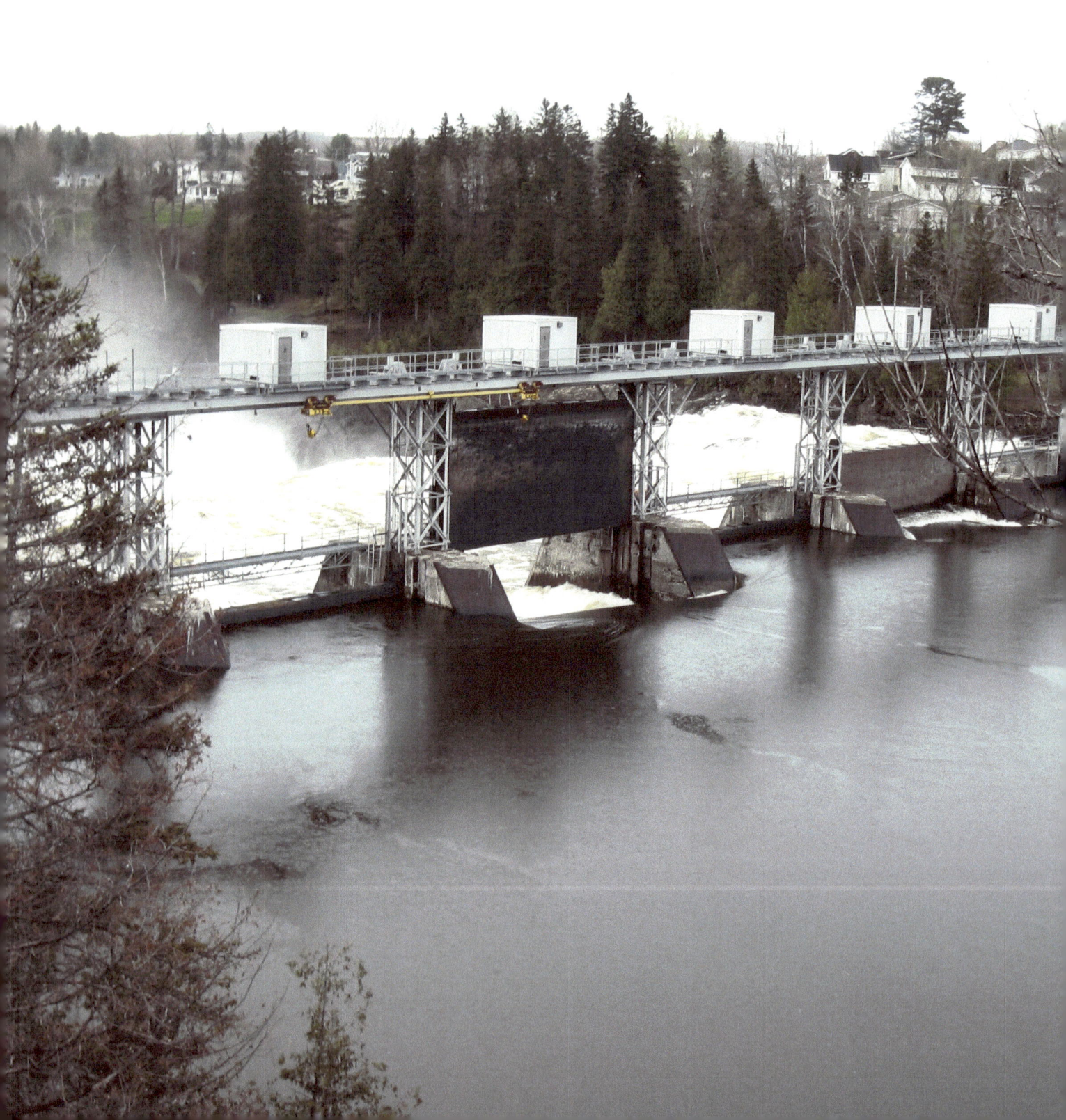

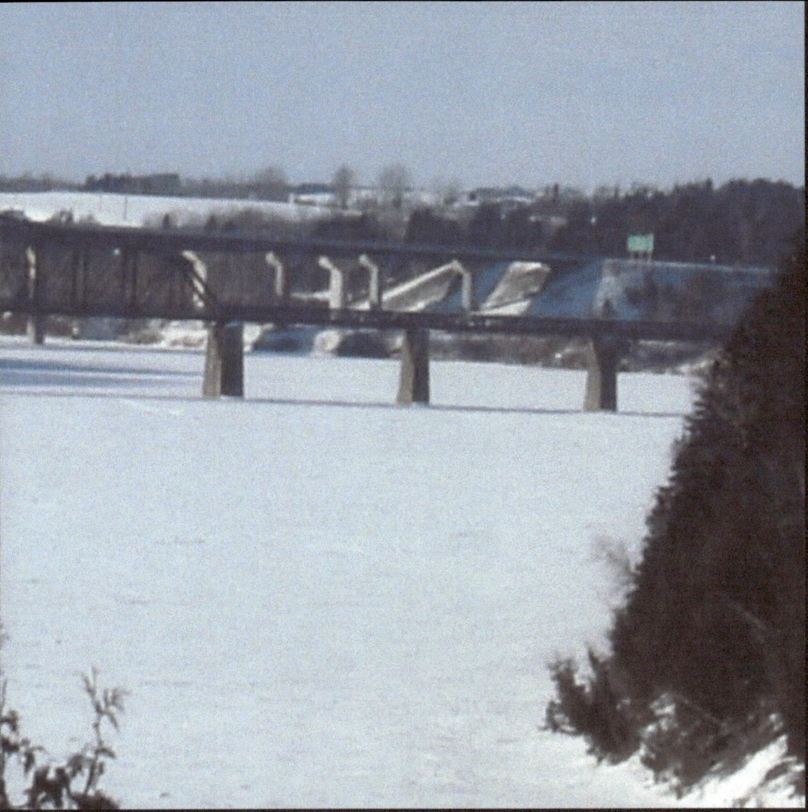

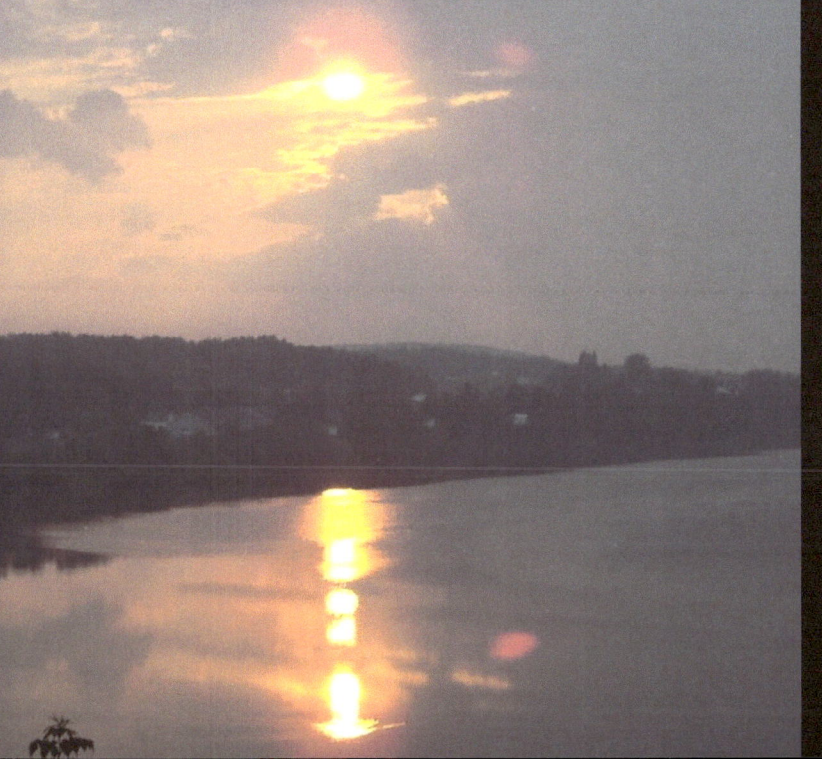

Arrière du Barrage

Behind the Dam

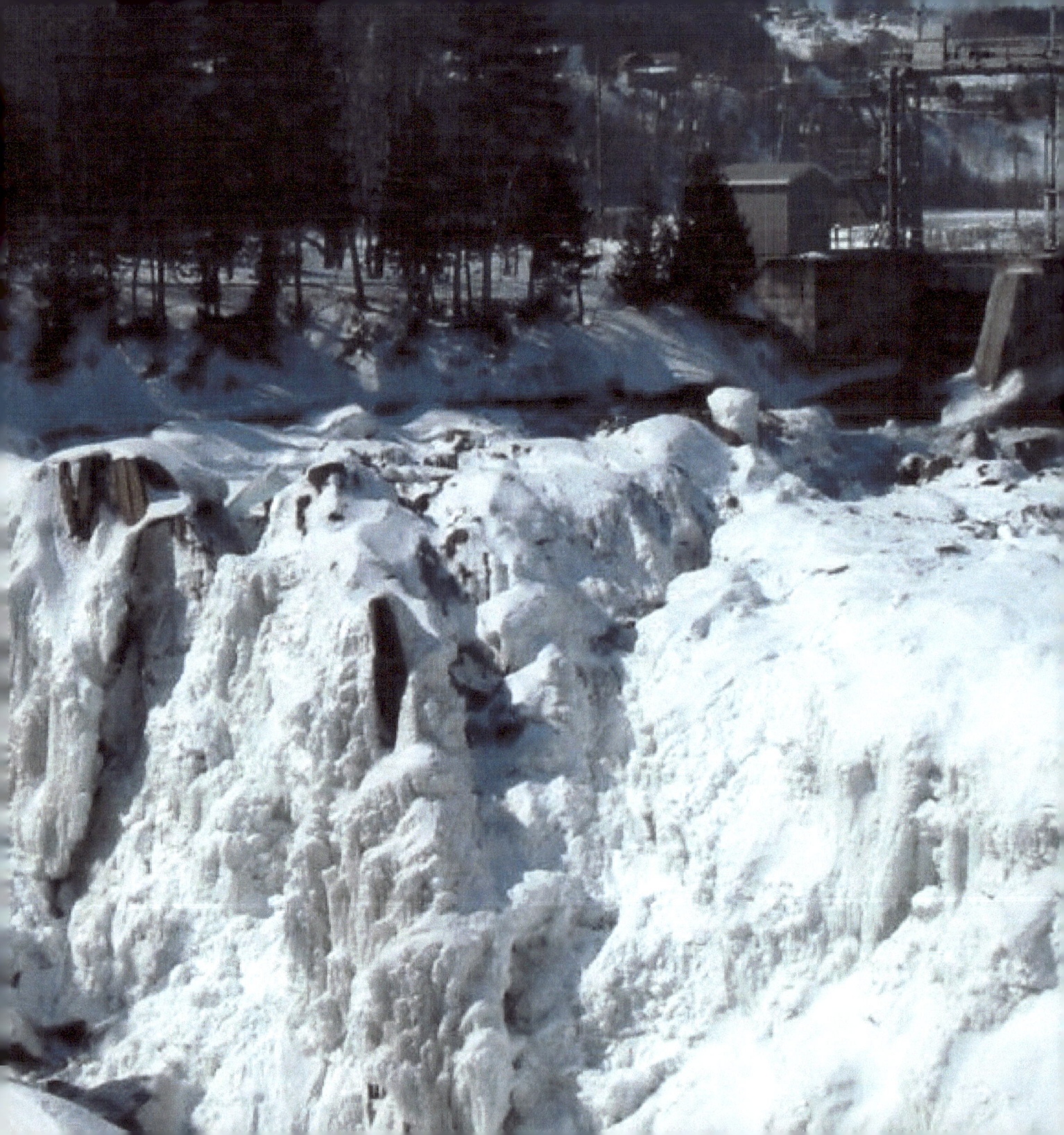

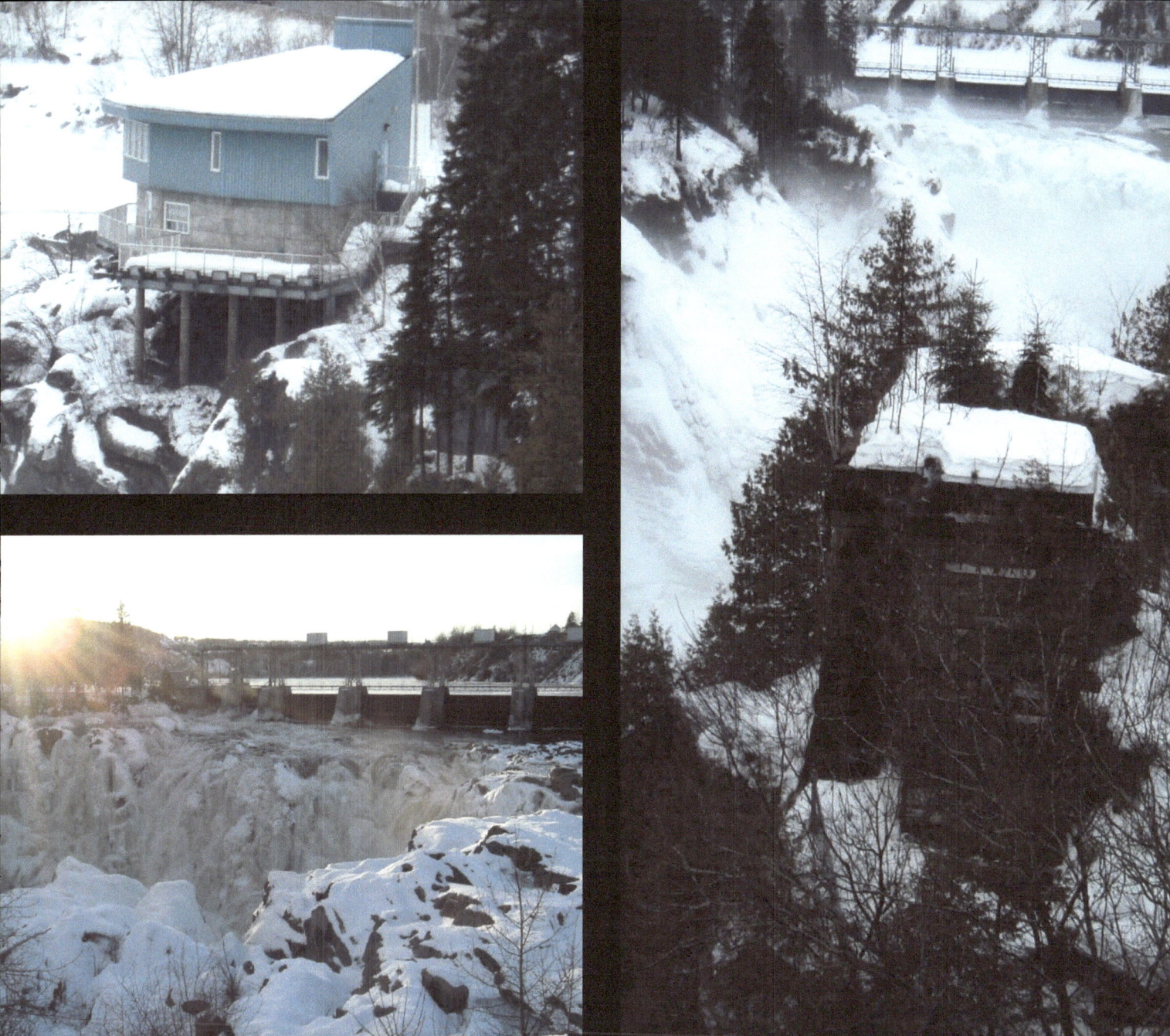

En Hiver
Winter

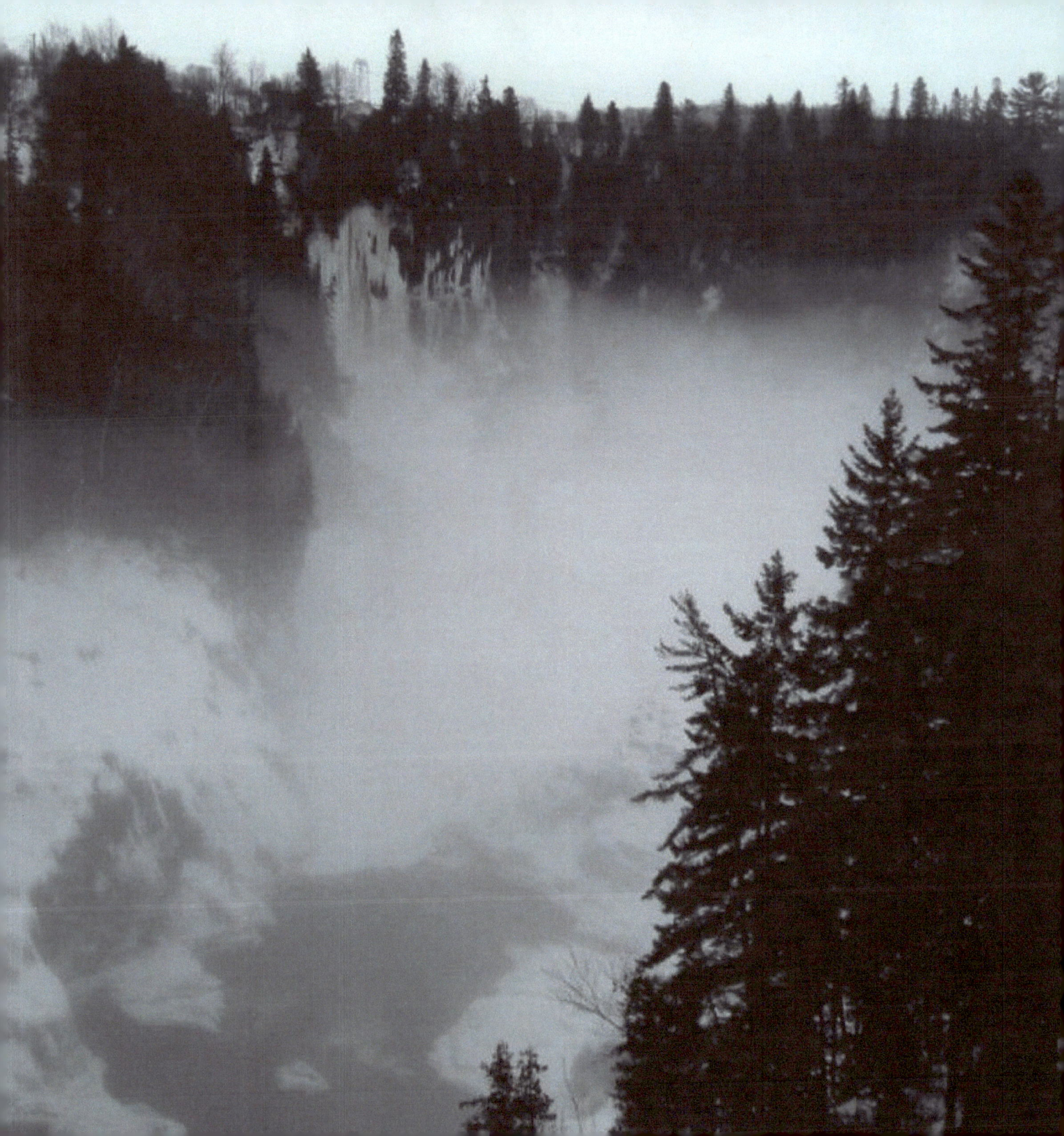

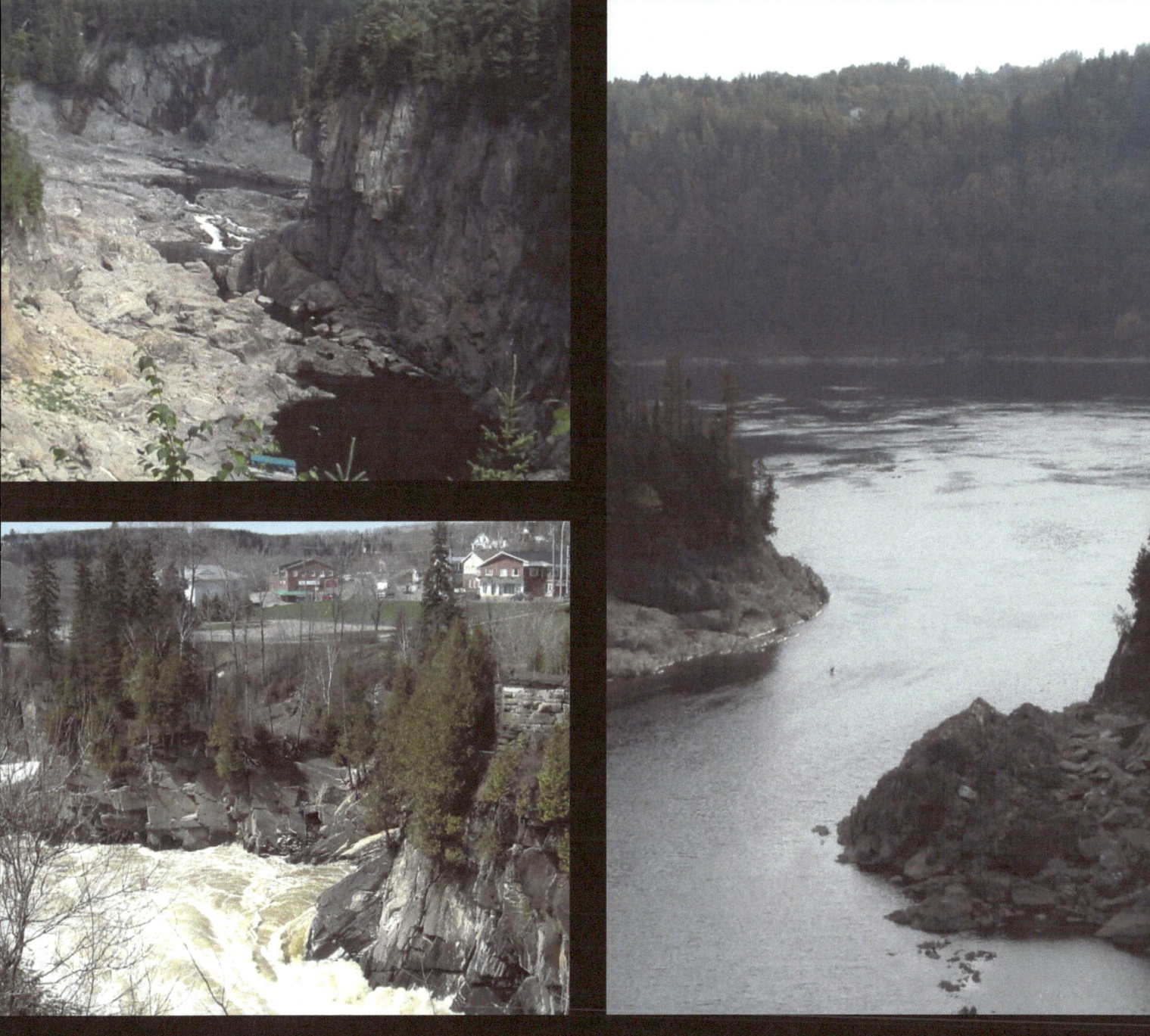

Le Gorge en Toutes Saisones
The Gorge in all Seasons

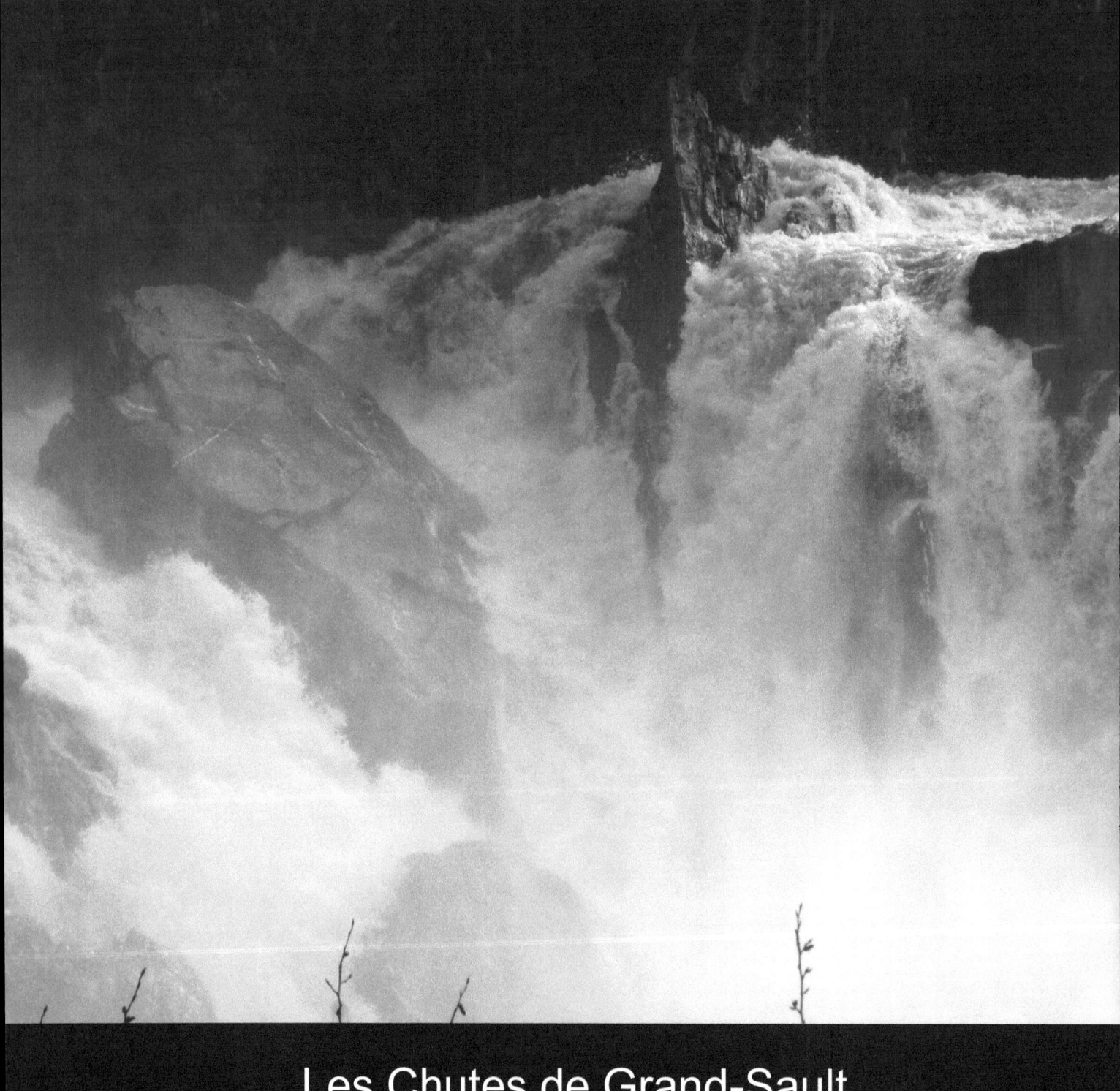
Les Chutes de Grand-Sault

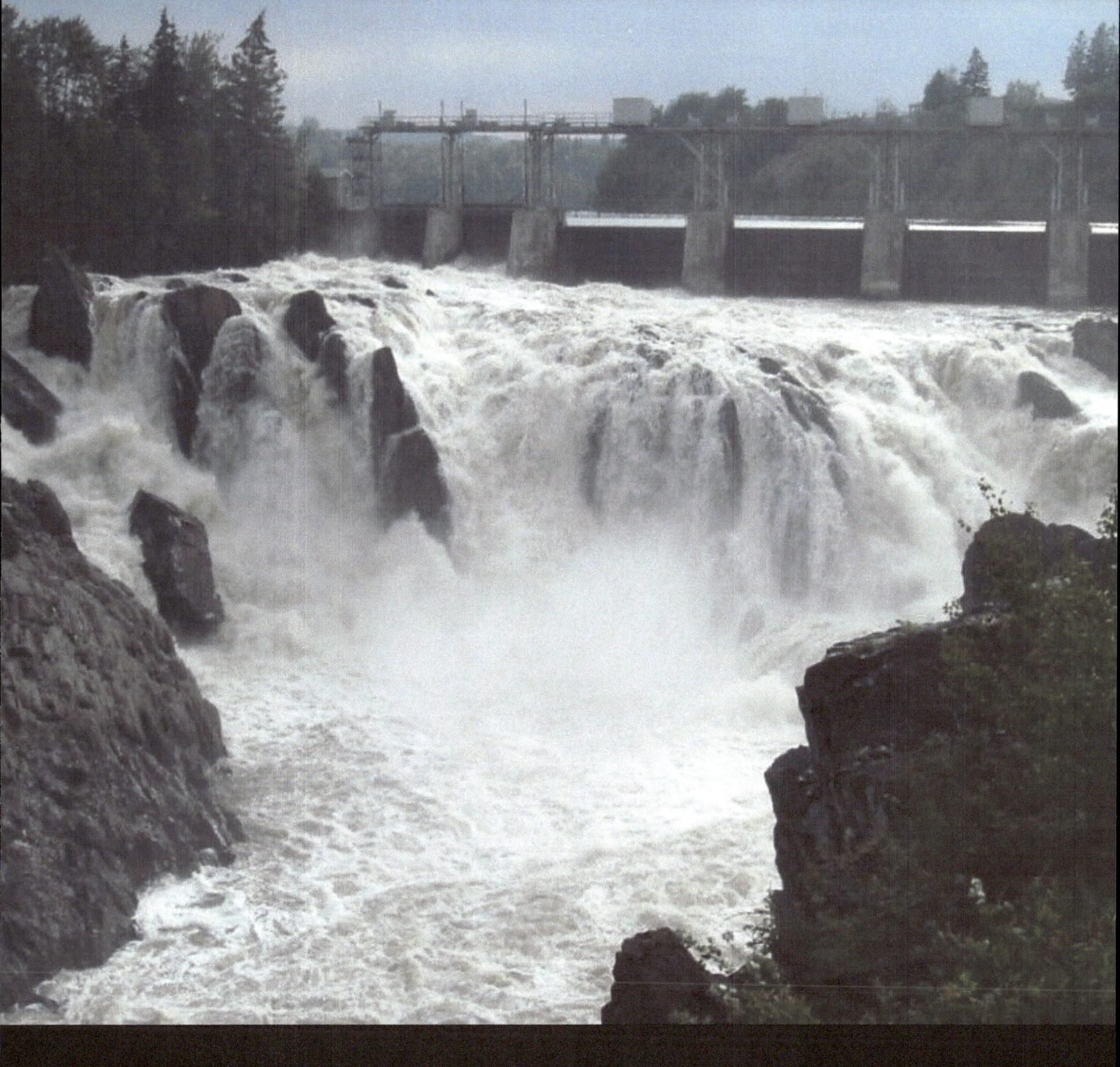
The Grand Falls

Wendy Koenig is a local author. Several of her works have won national awards. These photos were taken over the course of several years, 2005-2010.

www.ingramcontent.com/pod-product-compliance
Lightning Source LLC
Chambersburg PA
CBHW051835210526
45473CB00005B/1885